GOODNIGHT HUSBAND, GOODNIGHT WIFE

By Eric Stangel and Justin Stangel

Pictures by Adam J. Raiti

INSIGHT EDITIONS

San Rafael, California

In the green suburbs

There was a minivan

And a modest house

And a picture of–

Larry and Renee on their wedding day

And the girl and the boy who bring them such joy

Goodnight Wife
Goodnight photos of our old life

Goodnight thinning hair and head soon to be bare

Goodnight hairy back that needs a weed whack

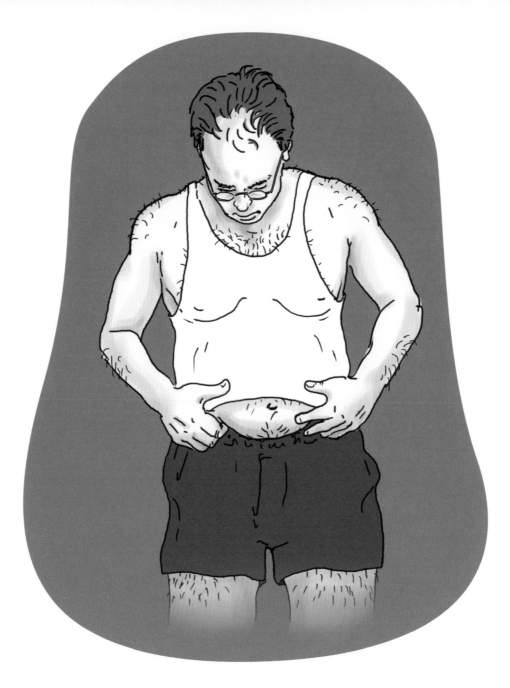

Goodnight six-pack abs and a body toned up

Hidden by a beer belly and a solid B cup

Goodnight childproofed house
locked tight with a *clink*

Since I can't open the toilet,
I take a leak in the sink

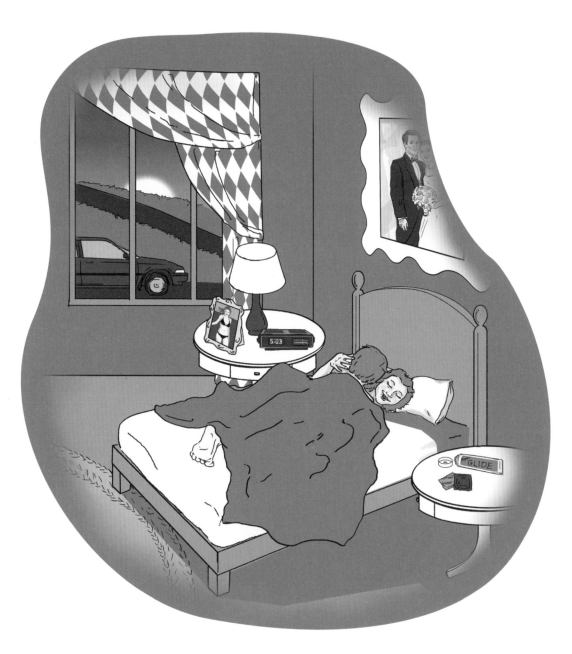

Goodnight making love 'til the sun did shine

Now we're watching Bravo and asleep by nine

Goodnight marijuana we used to keep in the drawer

These days the nightstand holds Viagra and Lipitor

Goodnight stain left by Kenny the pup
Now we both pretend not to see it
And hope the other cleans it up

Goodnight Dear, for whom I gave up my career

And my power suits and business plans

Now I drive around in a vomit-stained minivan

Goodnight beach vacations and tan complexion
I retired the bikini after my second C-section
E

Goodnight lingerie I'd wear for romance
Traded in for granny underpants

Goodnight evenings that were never boring

Barry White's been eclipsed by your nonstop snoring

Goodnight wild parties

That would bring the house down

Now "party" means a jumpy castle
And a creepy clown

Goodnight lofty dreams we used to dream

Replaced by online Scrabble and your fantasy team

Goodnight wiry hairs on my chin
When the hell did that begin?

Goodnight breasts once perky and butt once firm
That all went to hell once egg met sperm

Goodnight Husband

Goodnight Wife

Goodnight to our old life

But we wouldn't have it any other way

INSIGHT
EDITIONS

PO Box 3088
San Rafael, CA 94912
www.insighteditions.com

Library of Congress Cataloging-in-Publication Data available.

ISBN: 978-1-60887-093-6

This book is a parody and has not been prepared, approved, or authorized by the
creators of *Goodnight Moon* or their heirs or representatives.

Viagra® and Lipitor® are registered trademarks of Pfizer Inc.
Scrabble® is a registered trademark of Hasbro, Inc.

ROOTS of PEACE   REPLANTED PAPER

Insight Editions, in association with Roots of Peace, will plant two trees for each tree
used in the manufacturing of this book. Roots of Peace is an internationally renowned
humanitarian organization dedicated to eradicating land mines worldwide and converting
war-torn lands into productive farms and wildlife habitats. Together, we will plant two
million fruit and nut trees in Afghanistan and provide farmers there with the skills and
support necessary for sustainable land use.

Manufactured in China by Insight Editions

2 4 6 8 10 9 7 5 3 1

DEDICATION

ERIC: To my wife Liz and daughter Eva

JUSTIN: To my wife Lara and daughters Emily and Ashley

And to our parents Lois and John
We love you

Thanks for putting up with our crap